MOUTH & FRUIT

MOUTH & FRUIT

POEMS

CHRYSS YOST

GUNPOWDER PRESS • SANTA BARBARA
2014

Published by Gunpowder Press
David Starkey, Editor
PO Box 60035
Santa Barbara, CA 93160-0035

Back cover photo: George Yatchisin

ISBN-13: 978-0-9916651-1-2

www.gunpowderpress.com

For George

Dear Book,

I am going to read you
so hard. I am going to take
you home and hold your
open rigid spine in my hands
and read until your pages
are creased and smudged
like napkins after a feast,
finally fully sated.

ACKNOWLEDGEMENTS

Thank you to the editors and publishers who first gave home to these poems, including: *Askew, Bohemia, Crab Orchard Review, The Louisiana Review, The Hudson Review, Portnia, Quarterly West,* and *Tenemos.* Some poems were included in limited edition chapbooks: *La Jolla Boys* (Mille Grazie Press) and *Escaping from Autopia* (Oberon/Aralia Press).

"Furious Bread" was selected by Patricia Smith for the Patricia Dobler Poetry Award and appeared in *Voices from the Attic,* Volume XIX (Jan Beatty, ed.). Many of these poems were edited in residency at Carlow University.

Among the poems written as poet laureate of Santa Barbara, "Ember" was commissioned by Santa Barbara Hospice. "The Flow" commemorates the re-opening of the Cater Water Treatment Plant.

"Dear Book" was written to commemorate the opening of Granada Books in Santa Barbara. "Tribute" and "Postcard from Venice" were written as part of an artistic collaboration with the Santa Barbara Museum of Art, a strong supporter of poetry. "Old Habits" was commissioned by the Santa Barbara Museum of Natural History. "Seasonal" was created for the Visual Verse Project in collaboration with quilter Karin Carter.

"Considering the Rescue" was published in *The Fairest of Them All: An Anthology of Very Short Stories, Essays, and Poems Inspired by Snow White* (John Daniels, ed.). "Descanso, California" and "California Poem" were included in *The Geography of Home: California's Poetry of Place* (Chris Buckley and Gary Young, eds.).

All poems and the poet have been improved with long-standing support from Marsha de la O, Perie Longo, Glenna Luschei, John Ridland, Bruce Schmidt, Barry Spacks, David Starkey, Phil Taggart, and Paul Willis. Thanks also to Dana Gioia, David Oliveira, and M. L. Williams.

Contents

Tribute

I offer you these things, my living lord:
wildflowers baked in heavy bread,
a bouquet made of broken meadow birds,
a sculpture of the lovers' boats for rent
along the swirling edges of Charybdis—
one version of me waiting in each bow.

Uncarve me from this simple single skin,
your kisses, cupcakes hiding nail files,
the hinges from a dozen doors, and this
I offer you with open, floured hands—
to you, my purpose and my truest mate,
baking, waiting, lunging at the gate.

The First

I felt the darkness coming,
                    heard it crack,
whispering like saw-grass in the frost.

The exiles returning and the lost
            pacing, plotting, marking their way back.

At night the window locks us in.
            The black glass barely shows

that hurky dance that goes
            knocking leaves from bone-bare limbs.

Scales replace the summer softness,
            skin sloughing into rattles and hiss.

The year pares down to this.

Wicked

You are the swarm gathering force, collecting

and constructing. I feel the walls rise, warming, fragrant.

The wind stills. What need have we for windows?

This desire, the need of blossoms to be kissed,

for pollen mulled in the mouth like a poem

to be shaped into lotus pods, to be filled with seed,

to open in heat. Lucky wick, surrounded by softening

wax, sweet with the breath of bees.

O

Who can whisper the lascivious round
     without loosing the jaw, imagining softness?

O, wise universe, evolver of both mouth
     and fruit, sucked from the same dark ooze.

The pickers' hand, the weight of the nectarine,
     the tangelos, the ruby reds.

The earth was made in your image, Sphere,
     and we orbit because we are made

for those round things that nourish, that tempt,
     that make us clutch and bite for sweetness

     when the moon is a honeydew
        low in the morning sky.

Last Night

When the sun sets, and he isn't home, she walks
Not to be waiting, but she leaves a note:
Back soon, her only message, only wish.

After all, she didn't think he'd stay;
No plans, so no surprises when it ends.
The dishes wait unwashed. Bitter stains

Stretch like shadows on the tablecloth.
Once you believe in finding gods in men
You understand their restlessness as faith;

The way she feels his truth against her skin,
The rough edge of a matchbook, while she grieves
To see her saviors lost, and lost again.

God save the church that she takes refuge in,
The sanctuary given fools and thieves,
This silent girl who loves a man who leaves.

Furious Bread

The yeast wakes up, faster than sourgrass after the rain.
I warm the old bowl on the pilot light, as my grandmother did,

scrape level the measure of flour using a knife's flat back.
There is no end to stubborn in this world. Even flour

fights like it would rather be grain again, recoils after every stretch,
the dough thick and heavy as a lump of potters' clay.

I push hard, throwing my weight behind each stroke,
arms stiff, lifting on my toes. Flatten, fold, turn, flatten, fold.

The newspaper on the table shows a senator. Resolved,
he says. One man, one woman. His God will not be swayed.

I pound the kneading board, knead until my wrists ache,
my skin crusted with salt, slowly will *yield*, will *suppleness*.

I round the dough to rest in the deep glazed bowl,
wait for rising, baking, food for those who sit at my table.

All Hallows

Let the darkness sleeping in your bones
wake up late in autumn, with a howl.
Wake, and call the others from their homes.

Rattle from door to door and chant
a liturgy of need and want. We come
wearing our makeup and our masks.

We come dressed in clothes that we don't own.
We are phantoms, we are killers, we are clowns.
Let the darkness sleeping in your bones

creep out like a spider from its home.
We shriek. We moan. We rattle our chains.
We wake and knock and you unlock the door.

La Jolla Boys

We sit here on the pier and think
That, someday, we will drink.
We tip our Pepsi toward the sun
It's vintage 1981.
Still too young for real fun
And rich La Jolla Boys.

Me and Jenny planning through
Our string bikini beach debut
But haven't got a thing to flaunt
Against this sea of debutantes
Their fishing lines already taut
With rich La Jolla Boys.

As strong as Crystal Pier is long
And eyes Pacific blue,
We've waited more than fifteen years
To meet men just like you.
We practice doing runway walks
And suck on popsicles like cocks
And build sand castles as we talk
Of rich La Jolla Boys.

Motel 6

Eyes red, toes raw, chlorine blonde,
dangling her legs off the diving board,
she knows more than she should about
diving for pennies, timing her breath,
fighting boys who hold her under.

She divides the water with her fingertips,
finds the pulsing quiet six feet down
the broken sun on the surface above
and later her damp stomach pressed
against the warm concrete.

Otter, minnow, barracuda, shark, prophet
she has been to the bottom and back.
She swims as if there is no drowning,
as if there is no car in the parking lot
full of suitcases and paper bags.

Skeletown

I love the jingle jangle of the joints,
the bones untendoned and bright
the teeth will not stop smiling
no matter what got them all here.

These bones were made for dancin'
Rattling round to Shakedown St.
Old spooky toons with cat bones
chased by dog bones, collars on.

Look, I think to my aching frame,
how happy they all seem.
When I glimpse you in an x-ray,
it's looking in that freaky mirror.

I want that clacking bone joy
shining all the way through this thin
sullen and temporary skin.

Escaping from Autopia

but even leaving, longing to be back,
to do again what I did yesterday—
I, Miss Highway, I couldn't drive off track

or crash. I joined the candy-coated pack
to follow yellow lines and concrete, gray
but even. Leaving. Longing to be back

beyond those lines, in other lines. Like smack
these flashback rides, E-ticket crack: You pay
you have to stay. I couldn't drive off track,

or spin to face my enemies' attack.
The road signs told me "NOW LEAVING L.A."
but even leaving, longing to be back

to go again. I knew I had a knack
for getting there and going. Child's play,
and anyway, I couldn't drive off track,

once safety-strapped onto that strip of black.
I couldn't lose or get lost on the way,
but even leaving, longing to be back
and be okay. I couldn't drive off track.

Considering the Rescue

Maybe the princess didn't really sleep
through her entire sentence in that box.
Perhaps she peeked a little here and there,
maybe rubbed the foggy glass to gaze
now and then upon the grazing deer,

trading whistles with the mockingbirds.
Grumpy should have left a magazine.
A real princess, you insist, would wait
surrendered to the spell, allowing love
to save her from her temporary death.

Should I wait for hoof beats and a kiss?
Would it wreck the mood if I were here
all restlessness and heat and wide awake?
Must I pretend to sleep, for story's sake?

Westside

My house jingles in the city's hip pocket,

with the shaggy palms and the paleta man.

The street twists and constricts and we feed

the rats to it. Red and blue pits run loose,

growling with the pipes under the gritted

crossroads. This house wears its grassy caul,

gnashes its teeth to strangers.

It's your hood,

baby, says Pops. *When they rip it off your head,*

I say let them.

Childhood

Always a pool by the time we move out,
and weeks to splosh in a red clay pit
while workers curve rebar to fit. We put
on our bathing suits, bright pink and frilled,
and leap into the mud. We mug for the
camera, splay our redded palms, stick out
tongues. We make mud pies, mud roads,
mud houses before they line the shell
with sky-white cement, turquoise tiles at the lip.
It takes days to fill it with the garden hose.
Then we swim. Then we move.

Old Habits

I needed to renounce familiar things—
       I wasn't going away, I thought, but *towards*.
Now, pulled out of black waters,
       wet towels draped across my back,
my old home will not hold me anymore.

Who can teach a caterpillar joy
       when, comfortable with creeping, she must fly?
Craving leaves, she finds her teeth are gone
       and though her life has been a holding on
she no longer feels steady on her branch.
       When does she forget her other parts—
bright wrapping-paper wings around
           her hungry, crawling heart?

Wanted

Our sneakers on, we climbed outside—
pirates from portholes, grizzlies from dens—
a hidden fort in every hedge
and secrets like potato chips
in salty crumbs across our lips.
The hiss of Rainbirds at our heels.
Suburban summer battlegrounds
of shirts and skins and treachery.
Close to caught a hundred times,
we managed (just) to get away
and stay wanted one more day.

While all our playful years sneak past,
every wave of summer grass
taunts us in our offices
and scrapes the bottom of our cars
like silver hooks on drowning arms.
We drive with all the windows up
past the kids in vacant lots—
until the Wall Street news comes on,
they dart like fish beyond the glass.

Now silent on the porch, we toss
our secrets out like hand grenades
and watch them burn the emerald blades
of need and unfilled desires.

The fireworks that won't explode
twist and turn the driveway black.
We've made it home, but no one chases,
or seeks our secret hiding places.

Lanterns

A bowl of candies waits beside our door.
Or *my* door—not ours anymore.
After the cleaning part, the scraping out,
the seeds are drying in the stove
and when it's time to carve,
the face cut from the hollowed shell
makes me think of who we were,
flickering and unintentionally cruel.

The little ones come by six o'clock.
Hour by hour, the children grow taller
and their costumes almost disappear.
There wasn't time to close the door
between the knocks some years,
but this has been the emptiest October.
Even *we* is not the word it used to be,
when you were part of us, and me.

Terzanelle in Blonde

Some things can be changed. Not yesterday
And not your leaving me. I'll dye my hair.
This blonde is too much yours for me today:

Too long and sentimental, unaware.
The insistent "if" of blonde, and "then,"
And not "you're leaving me." I'll dye my hair,

Until it's black as yours, and then again.
I'll dye until it's red or grey, to drown
The insistent "if" of blonde, and then

Your words becoming tied to hers, the sound
Of lovers' voices. Should be mine with yours.
I'll dye until it's red or grey, to drown

The echo of your whispers on my shoulders,
Saturate the swish of my own heart,
Of lovers' voices. Should be mine with yours

Tangled up for days, not torn apart.
Some things can be changed. Not yesterday,
Not your leaving, not the hardest part.
This blonde is too much yours for me today.

Cocktails

I sit on your patio, alone,
my empty glass as heavy as a gun,
my satin straps and clasps not yet undone.

Each guest shines with candlelight and wine
poised before the windows, drink in hand,
balanced on your perfect baritone.

This empty glass is just a timing gun:
a heavy heart, all steel and no shot,

that announces the anticipated start,
says it's time, at last, to run,

and takes the blame for blasting it apart.

Nothing in the Classifieds

Except for that one message (meant for whom?)
"I'm sorry. Take me back." And nothing else,
but I knew exactly how that felt.
Was it waiting there for me? Who wrote it? You?

The "Lost" column is longer than the "Found."
A wedding ring gone missing. Please return.
Reward for the old dog who ran away
Can Sit and Get the paper. Cannot Stay.

Free to good home doesn't mean for me.
I'm the kind that says, "I'm sorry. Take me back."
I have to read to know what people want,
a wailing wall, these little paper prayers.

Uncertainty

There is a hope insisting to be named.
Soon, one of us will be proven right.
You, my sweetheart. You, my big mistake.

When pregnant with my daughter I was warned:
Bad luck to those who name an unborn child.

I couldn't keep myself from calling her
a dozen names to help her find her home.

How difficult to settle on just one.
What happened to the other girls I named,
possibilities that I both made and missed?

No one knows disaster by its voice
but we listen for it. We might be the first.

Death, the Mob Boss

Death, I'm hoping you see this celebration
as our way to honor you. A season of respect.

When I see yet another naughty nurse I could
agree that at times it looks like mocking.

Grinning ghosts. Skeletons and candy gore.
The creepies and the crawlies made cute.

Death, no one wants to see you angry.
Not us. Not the naughty nurse.

Maybe especially not the nurse.

Road Song

It's another ride in the passenger's seat,
humming as the rear-view sunsets fade.
The landscape, like the radio, sings
familiar songs you didn't choose.
With the compromises you have made
a least you might enjoy the views.

How can you sit back and take this ride
as though you know the man who holds the wheel?
Wherever it is that you finally arrive
you will look behind you in the mirror
and wish the sunset hadn't disappeared

as if you could have driven it to stay
with your own foot hovering above the brake.

Penelope in Malibu

It's not easy being Mrs. Mr. Big;
      if you want grateful, marry ugly,
      if you want constant, marry blind.

You sign up for the summer-day parades,
      practicing the perfect matron's wave,
      but lipsticked masses press their faces

against the windows of your banquet hall,
      fogging up the view. So this is envy,
      a thousand understudies, waiting in the wings.

There are many ways that girls change into monsters:
      their hair hisses underneath the golden highlights
      and their Italian heels snap like vicious dogs.

His secretaries younger, meetings later,
      you rage like a suburban Juno at desire
      and the traffic crawling westward on Olympic.

Every singer chants *love is going, going, gone,*
      and there's no one to invoke to stop his leaving.
      No curse or prayer will stall this slow unweaving.

Scissors

They should keep them in hotels, part of the mini bar,
so you could drink two tiny Makers' Marks and a few other
of those cute little bottles and think, so far from the mirror
in your bathroom at home that knows how to talk you down,
you'd think, *A haircut—that's it!* because the hotel room says,
We're not asking you to move here, we have standards,
and it's true you packed for comfort and maybe you should
have been willing to pay a little to bring clothes that look,
well, make you look a little more, you know, *dressed,*
but there's no helping that now and shopping at this hour,
you know everything's closed, but your hair, hey, there's something
you can do something about, here's a pair of scissors, see
this is the way, on the front of this magazine, youthful, smart—
see if you can do something to fix yourself before it gets too late.

Lai with Sounds of Skin

Shall we dress in skin,
our living linen?
Bone weft,
pull of masculine
into feminine,
the heft,
the warp, weave and spin
of carded days in

tightly-twisted thin
yarns that we begin—
like wool
like *will*, like *has been*,
spoken to silken—
to spool:
thick bolts of linen,
skein to skin to skin.

Pruning

The plum gnarls its way through
the fall, bark splitting out resin
when the days get honeyed
with late heat. It will die this way,
slowly if we let it, rivered
by beetles and blight.
The rough, sick topography
when we finally get the saw,
tired of the wet plum rot.
The weather of each day
mapped into the branches
stacked to dry on the hearth,
logs that sing in winter's fires,
songs of sweetness and fruit.

Seasonal

It is summer and I want to stay in bed,
Our springtime is behind me.
Autumn will be next.

The grass whispers out
a long green breath.
Peaceful would
be one way
to describe this
sudden quietness.

The sheets ripple
as if I am a stone
dropped into them.
I pretend to be serene
but it feels like being alone.

Summer sings its soft blue song.
I close my eyes and listen to its words.
Fall waits while summer slowly disappears.

The Compulsion to Map

Though wrong, the atlas will outlast us.
While the lines define the gone Bombay
and Persia nuzzles the Khazar Sea,
this map insists the vanished
still exist, known by fading names.
It was true, but isn't, snapshot of a fact
evaporating. Constantinople licking Marmara,
speaking Turkish, Farsi, Greek.

No exception, the map of your own tongue—
regions once labeled *savory, sour, tart*
melt away and shift like any myth:
bitterness that lurks deep in the throat
salted like the edges of the sea,
tongue that flavors the voice,
sweetness that looses the jaw,
words that entered the world
singing their own names.

Flame Lessons

Maybe kindling
is a kind of kindness,
another way of warming.

And maybe kin
are a kind of kiln,
a womb, the cured clay

hardened in fire,
can break but cannot
crumble.

What was culled
was weak and incandescent
like a strange kiss.

Ash and sweeping,
spectacular sunsets.
All that's left of fire.

California Poem

"Another body found off Sunrise Highway, mouth filled with dirt."

His arm grew heavy on me as he slept, the oaks'
grey branches scratching the roof of the Chevy.
He drove right past my exit, east on 8,
not stopping as we curved in the mountains.
The morning was still cool and wet, my wrists
bound tight, my throat grown tight,
I pretended to sleep in California,
where poison oak was red already
the river stretched out thin across its bed.

The miners grab the river with both hands,
up and downstream, where my stiff arms point.
Hush, hush, hush, the gravel circles shallow pans
and we search, sift, sink deep into California.

At swimming holes, I used to take my shoes off
and let the river take my feet beneath the glittered silt,
take my ankles, calves, take the parts of me that you
called yours on my last night. I let the river weave
itself into my hair, then lay out in the sun,
half asleep, half awake, lay my body down
within the mountains. I felt my pulse
carve through the sandstone wash.

Now I hear the ocean through these hills,
The river in my mouth, this taste of gold.

50

The Old Bridge

Each summer, there were more planks gone.
The redwood pilings were pocked with acorns,
but we cousins would risk the crossing
barefoot, feeling like steelworkers perched on girders,
if just five feet above the slow, shallow Sweetwater.
At the center, I would belly down and stare
through the holes in the bridge to the water.
This was the line that squiggled along River Road
on the map, where the bridge was still a line you could drive on.
Somehow, in this stripe of mud, trout. Somehow,
this ribbon grew huge and hungry and ripped
it apart. Then emptied. And we stopped going
where the bridge would take us.

Descanso, California

The rich, black humus, airborne, glimmers gold,
gray granite boulders softly wrapped in moss
beneath the dusty light of oaks as old
as California.
                              Creeks just right to cross
with one wide leap and lined with cottonwood,
river stone chimneys, an abandoned bridge
which finally lost its lumber in the flood.

Manzanitas, red beneath the ridge,
the muted clop of horses down the street
melts the whispered rasp of raking leaves
filtered slowly through the mountain heat
beneath the stellar blue of make-believes:

        The slumber of Descanso's summer spell
        wrapped in a heritage of chaparral.

No Rain, No Water

In World War II, Santa Barbara sent out all its soldiers,
gathered up resistant poets in a Civilian Service camp
along the Santa Ynez River. They were told to tend the forest.
Only a poet could see a forest in the rough shrubs
of Los Padres, dry and hot from years of drought.
Two bucks a month—not Canada, jail or killing—to take
the nonsense work that they dealt out. Like building a bridge
on shrunken Lake Cachuma, where the shoreline has
remapped itself in mud. The poets know the bridge
will be underwater with the season's rains,
but this is war. No one complains.

The Flow

When the water comes, it brings the mountain
and sings the story of the shifting ridge,
summons green to bloom along its edge.
Shapes the hills with patient excavation.

Water comes and carries what we were:
wind-torn leaves, the old path washed away,
the swallowed reflections of hunter and prey.
Brings ash and remains of the bear flag bear.

When water comes, thirst rises for reunion
with the river. All are sullied by the journey.
What blessing to reclaim our purity,
leave the salty stories for the ocean.

We are renewed, to wonder which came first:
that flow of water or this endless thirst?

Finding the Nest

Our black hen wanders loose.
        Her eggs are cinnamon brown,
    but when the days are short
           she doesn't lay. It's been weeks
              since we found a nest.

You promised to keep checking
       when I left Santa Barbara.   A woman in Pittsburgh
           calls eggs *blanquillos*:
              Little white things.

Alone in my hotel, I am eating avocado,
      the pit like a little egg. I think of that space between
   our avocado tree and fence, tomorrow
           I'll ask you to look.

Advice for Women

Keep focused on the ceiling and you might
not bite your cheek too hard at the trespass
of cold metal sliding in. And you're right
to feel so pale and exposed (no mas-
ter of your body now!) Clinical light
keeps you composed here, but beyond the glass

window, in the lab next door, a glass
dish cultivates the worst in you. You might
give up the God you heard about in Mass
for antioxidants. There's time to right
your wrongs, and settle scores, before you pass
like breath remade as clouds by winter light

in sharp still mornings. Fluorescent light
rains down on you like blue-white sun in glass
test tubes, like luminescent dynamite.
The gossiping of cells is like a mass
of schoolgirls, watching in the hallway, right
before you stumble. Make small talk to pass

the time. Forget the test, of course you'll pass.
They look for microscopic faults with light
that radiates right through the you on glass.
They'll set aside the parts of you that might
grow into something more. They might amass
more samples, to be sure that you're all right.

Because of course you are. Even if, right
after she turned twenty, my aunt passed
on, mossy black inside her like a mite-
infested paper-white narcissus, glass-
forced to root in a window's filtered light.
Too many women in this family, mas-

sacred by cancer rushing them en masse,
as they stood stunned, slashing left and right,
killing and leaving the rest afraid. Passed
on like a recipe, along with light
blue eyes, fears as strong and old as sea glass.
I want to be like them; I fear I might.

For now, breathe lightly as the forceps pass.
A mass is a mass, no more . . . Later, write
about the fate that might be held in glass.

Mattress Tags

In 1910, with the smallpox still
at work, the deads' mattresses
were gutted   re-covered,
          sold as clean.
Under coarse blankets
          lurking in the ticking
                    virus

TO EXTEND LIFE, FLIP MATTRESS

says a label on my brand-new bed.
Please, mattress, don't smuggle sorrow
into my home or allow fear to burrow
beside me at night.

ALL NEW MATERIALS / DO NOT REMOVE

as if it's easy to upset my intention to sleep in this familiar shape.
as if it's easy to prevent that quick slip from languorous to lonely.

Even during sleep I grow more
set into myself. Each creek insists
          on carving out its bed and I wear down
                    a rut against the springs.

This mattress will hold no one
          after me.

Most Importantly, That

Amazed in waves by the world,
agog how simple it is to create,
from nothing, an apple. It's just seed
and time, water, sun, and soil.
After a few years, the blossoms,
the bees, and the small fruit.
How little it took for this majesty
to be here, scattering the ground
with fruit, the air scented with cider,
and inside the house, you love me.

Beachcombing in Pittsburgh

    The salt here
               looks like sea glass.
The melted snow
               must taste like ocean.
    Rivers thaw
               and I miss the Pacific.
    Sometimes
               we run the beach at home
  the sand seems
               made of tiny shells
    that crunch
               just like snow-salt
  and the waves
               sound like a car
in melting snow.
               I am a shell
    desperately
               layering.

Postcard from Venice

I've fallen in love today. My gondolier
Sang me operas at sunset and my souvenir
Is the sky over Venice, now tinted with peach.
He steered past the windows of bedrooms where lovers
looked down on the water, like saints from a niche,
blessing the gondolier keeping their cover.
I thought of you, darling, as I stepped to the pier.
Do you like Verdi? I wish you were here.

Three Tracks from *London Calling*

1. Rudy Can't Fail

What the heck is feckless?
From the back, that jackass
was just another crackhead.
I've watched them kick
their thick black boots
with no thought for work.

Chug it, you fucking slacker.
There's a jab and a smack
asking for you out back.

2. Guns of Brixton

This whole place has been blasting open
since before it was a place, before there
was a surface to the earth. Violence
what we're made of. We are stardust,
tarnished and repelled by the rest
our own dusty breath. God is a bullet.
The rest of us, we're nothing but targets.

3. Lover's Rock

It's all about possession, singular.
And for what you do with your girl,
you barely need to like her at all.
It's not for smashing out plans,
just a place to take off her pants.
Far from your goddam parents,
but just far enough to go all the way.
Just rock. No lovers here today.

Pumpkin

After a long season of tending,
I am no farmer. The meager harvest
all the more precious in count. To cut
the vine that roiled over the planter
in its prime, now brittle with a hair
of needles—how can one just cut?
The courage to cull, then slice open
that sparse bounty, to ruin with a slice
all chance of preserving the flesh.
Pumpkin, all summer I promised
you would be the diva of October
and you are, gutted and illuminated,
the grinning harvest we chose
not to eat and not to have.

Dia de Los Muertos

For most suburban white girls,
                ghosts come to life
        in slumber party mirrors,
                      but I was born into a haunted house.

Maybe I belong with the sugar-skull crew,
        ladies with faces like bone,
                penciled grins,
        coal sunken eyes,
                fiesta blouses loose around brown shoulders.

I've seen spirits darkening the corners,
                      rattling the bedframe as I sleep.
        I was born with banshee in my blood,
                  a fierce madness
                  when the wind shifts.

Fearless *muertas*, flirting with the band,
        I've got my heels on.
        Come dance, La Llorona,
                the living weep enough.

Echocardiogram

They monitor my etch-a-sketchey pulse.
My heart, a gray fist on the screen,
still inside my body. Thump thump.
Thump thump. There I am. And when
the image freezes, am I there too?
Gasping, ending, screen heart stopped?
A bigger shock not to see you there,
where I was sure you had carved
a home, where I feel you most.

Grain

Across the lot,
the field oats
are white where
they were chopped
or bent beneath the heat.

Only these few remain to seed,
to pass the story of what was risen,
remain to grow and ripen,
still unchosen.

Ember

The memory of you is light, a fire

that warms and flares. The spark

we shared later charred

me hollow. At times I felt scarred,

rough and brittle, by the inferno

of sorrow like a gnarled black oak,

baring my limbs to the great star.

You have been fuel and smoke.

The way of loss is the way of fire:

ravenous, illuminating. Hot glare

that yields flames to an ember.

There is no cure, no knowing

as loss furrows when it will go.

We only witness the bright flicker,

celebrate feeling this gentle glow,

what wild, untouchable light you were.

Already Gone

Screw you and your second chance—
        The regrets of the dead are conceits of the quick.
Resurrection may be rescue in romance,

fine for Princess Lacey and Prince Satin-Pants,
        but consider the sated, the tired, the sick,
the downright done with living askance—

Called back from some cheap enchantment.
        Over my dead everything, you prick.
How unreassuring resurrection seems.

Encore! then forced re-entrance...
        Let the dead move on, have their plans,
let them choose their cans and can'ts.

Only the quick wish the dead awake.
        Screw you and your second chance.
Fuck your resurrection scams.

Breath

Oh my breath, how I feel you leave my body
as if you were made of silk, pulled through my throat.
Magicians, how they feel their mortality over and over
like tailors fingering a hem, rubbing for knots
hidden on the inner seam. I know you will leave
me with a rough jag of thread a-dangle
as I feel the cough coming on, and my chest
seizing tight, the yardage aching its way loose
like a kite string through the fingers of a child.

Mooring

How to gauge this day and all its distances
before the fog has had its chance to lift?

With each dark wave, the shoreline shifts,
the water slowly licking through the rock.

Her kiss that is consumption and caress
dissolving this ephemeral grey *yes*.

Do you feel your destination drawing close?
Is this the harbor you were meant to choose?

We live this day, not knowing where it goes.

One Hand Holding

Barry is getting ready to go. That's all you Buddhists do:
say goodbye and goodbye from your cushions, until your eyes
stay cool and hooded no matter who they farewell. You practice

leaving until it's like walking outside, going to the kitchen
for a little something, flipping a channel. Calm changing,

no matter what unenlightened stomps and howls come
from the ones left in this newly barren world. Stones,
smooth and solid, below the currents of water. Barry,

I would love you by being a stone, by being a branch
on the bank, but you know I am foolish and graspy.

All I feel tonight is drowning. Wanting your hand.